Communicating in Colour

T0364527

Contents

Written by Inbali Iserles

Collins

1 Changing colour

Some animals have an incredible skill –
like a superpower! They can change
their colour. An octopus does
this in the blink of an eye,
switching not only
the shade of its skin, but
also its **texture** from
smooth to bumpy.

Arctic foxes change more slowly. Once a year, they **shed** their famously snowy white coats for brown ones.

Golden tortoise beetles turn red when **stressed**.

Best known of all are chameleons – lizards that go through many amazing colour changes.

Why do animals do this? The answer is not as simple as it seems.

Colour is important in the animal world. In this book, we will **investigate** how animals use colour to:

- blend in: using **camouflage** to hide from **predators**
- stand out: as a warning to others
- stand out: to attract a **mate**.

4

Tiny golden tortoise beetles are usually **metallic** gold. They turn red when worried to scare off predators.

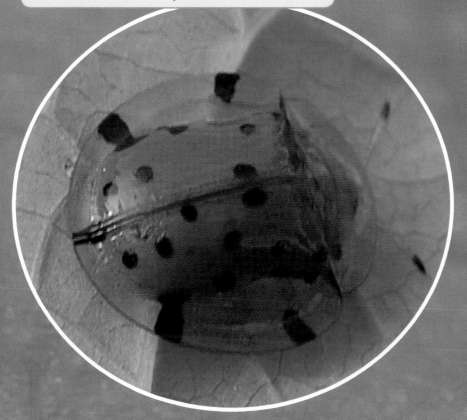

The dramatic colour change of golden tortoise beetles hints at another way that animals use colour. Can you think what that might be?

2 Camouflage

Why would an animal use camouflage?

Being able to hide your appearance can mean the difference between life and death. If you're a predator, camouflage makes you better at hiding and more likely to catch your prey. If you're being hunted, camouflage can help you hide from predators.

Animal case study

Children's stick insect from Australia look so much like the eucalyptus leaves where they hide that they're very hard to spot!

Blending in

Camouflage usually means that animals have skin, fur, scales or feathers with similar colours or **markings** to their **environments**.

Animal case study

With their patterned brown feathers, great horned owls look a lot like the trees where they nest. This protects them from predators. Camouflage also makes the owls better at hiding from prey until the moment they swoop.

Disruptive camouflage

Instead of copying the colours or textures of their environment, some animals use colours or patterns that cleverly confuse the way others see them. This is called "disruptive camouflage".

When might disruptive camouflage be useful?

Where does one zebra end and another begin?

Animal case study

The lions that hunt zebras are part colour blind, so blending in wouldn't work. Zebras are **herd** animals. Their stripes make it hard for lions to focus on a single animal.

Disruptive camouflage means that individual members of a herd can hide even though they are in full view.

Animal case study

Young white-tailed deer have white spots on their brown backs. When they sit very still in tall grass, the spots look like sunlight through the trees, blurring their outline and hiding them from predators.

Do predators use disruptive camouflage? If you are strong and dangerous, why might you want to hide?

Animal case study

Big cats like leopards and tigers use disruptive
camouflage to help them hunt without being seen.
Leopards' spots help them hide in the **dappled** shade of
African forests and **savannah**, while tigers' stripes "blur"
against the red earth and grasses of the Asian jungle.

3 Seasonal camouflage

Some animals go one step further – they change in different seasons to fit in with their **surroundings**. This is seen in species of animals around the Arctic Circle. These animals change from brown in summer to white in winter.

arctic fox

arctic hare

white-tailed ptarmigan bird

In winter, the Arctic is covered in snow. In spring, much of the snow melts to reveal earth and rocks. A hare that blends in is less likely to be eaten. A fox in camouflage can sneak up on its prey.

Arctic winters are dark, while Arctic summer days are long and bright. Scientists believe that a change in the amount of light sends a message to the animal's body that it is time to shed its fur or feathers in preparation for the new season.

Animal case study

Siberian hamsters are sometimes kept as pets. If put in a room with plenty of year-round light, their snowy white fur becomes dark.

Not all **seasonal** colour changers are birds and mammals from the frozen north.

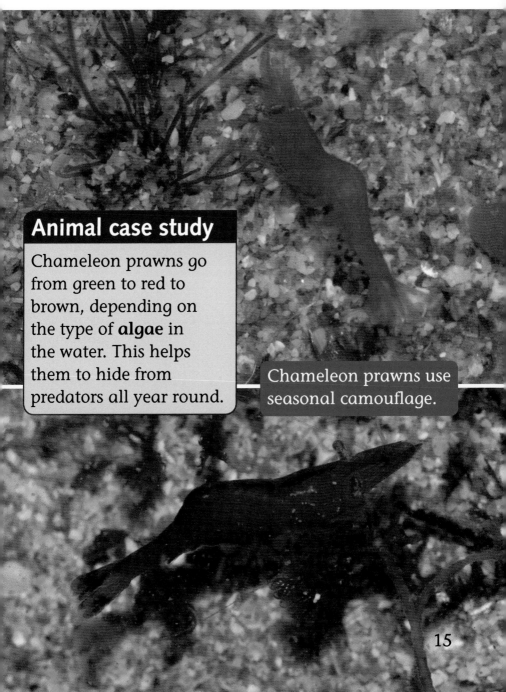

Animal case study

Chameleon prawns go from green to red to brown, depending on the type of **algae** in the water. This helps them to hide from predators all year round.

Chameleon prawns use seasonal camouflage.

4 Super-fast camouflage

Many fish are experts in blending or blurring to avoid being caught, and some can even change colour.

Animal case study

Flounders are a type of fish that change to blend in with the sea floor. Tropical flounders can change to match their background in two seconds!

Animal case study

The octopus is a master of disguise. It can change its skin colour and texture. This intelligent sea creature does not have bones in its body, so it can twist its shape as it changes its colour and texture.

Moment to moment, an octopus can copy a rock, the sea floor or a coral reef.

5 Danger! Do not touch!

Many animals spend their lives hiding from predators. But some species do the opposite – they try to stand out.

Creatures such as snakes, frogs, butterflies and fish use warning colours to scare off predators. These animals are poisonous, and eating them would lead to sickness or even death. Their bright colours send a warning to leave them alone.

poison dart frog

Animal case study

Poison dart frogs are the most **venomous** creatures on Earth. A single frog could kill ten adult humans!

monarch butterfly

spined lionfish

banded krait

19

Humans see a lot of colours. Birds see even more! Their sight gives them extra depth, detail and **contrast**, and they can see ultraviolet, a colour that is invisible to us without special glasses. This gives birds a fantastic understanding of the world below them as they fly through the sky – great for spotting insects, and for noticing danger signs.

How animals see colour matters. Warning signs aren't much use if predators can't see them.

Some predators can't see some or all colours. For example, dogs – unlike humans – can't see red. Surely warning colours only work if predators can see them?

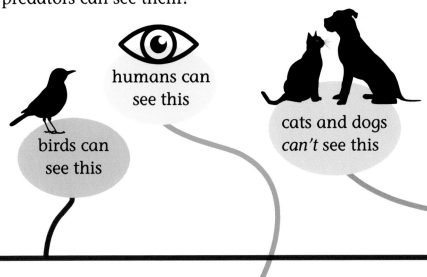

humans can
see this

birds can
see this

cats and dogs
can't see this

ultraviolet

In fact, colours may not matter as much as contrasts between them. Scientists did experiments with large, colour-blind insects called praying mantises. They found that the mantises learnt to avoid eating bitter-tasting bugs painted in different shades of grey. It seems that even if predators are colour blind, they can see the contrast between colours and this is enough to warn them.

colours humans can see

colours dogs can see

pit vipers can't see this either

but they can "see" this

infrared

6 Copycats

Warning colours tell predators, "Don't eat me,
I'm poisonous!" A bird that has been stung by
a wasp quickly learns to recognise the yellow body
and black stripes.

Some animals that are not poisonous use warning
colours to trick predators. They often look a lot like
other creatures that are poisonous. But they are
quite harmless!

Animal case study

Hoverflies are often yellow with black stripes.
They look a lot like bees and wasps, but they have
no sting!

Look at these two snakes. Both are covered in warning colours: red, yellow and black. One is highly poisonous; the other is harmless. Can you guess which is which?

The snake at the top is the harmless scarlet king snake. It **mimics** the poisonous coral snake to scare off predators.

We have seen how octopuses are brilliant at camouflage. Amazingly, one species of octopus is also a master mimic. Changing to look like the reef or the sea floor may be fine for an octopus when it's staying still, but what about when it has to swim through open water?

Mimic octopuses cover their arms in black and white bands, trailing them behind like the poisonous spines of a lionfish. They can also copy other sea creatures.

spined lionfish

Octopuses use disguise to hide from predators, or to pretend they're poisonous. They also use their fantastic range of colours to look **attractive**! Standing out can get you noticed by a mate.

Let's see how other animals use colours to look good.

mimic octopus

7 Getting noticed

Have you ever stopped by a shop to look at a colourful window display? Or wondered why sweets are usually bright colours like pink, yellow and green?

Bright colours make us look again, and humans aren't the only ones that do this.

Many animals like bright colours. They use them to attract a mate.

Animal case study

Male peacocks do not blend in – especially when they want to attract females. They raise their **shimmering** tail feathers like a giant fan.

Female peacocks – peahens – are mostly brown, blending with the forest and **bushland** habitats where the birds live.

To attract a mate, male birds of paradise have to stand out. Bright, glossy feathers help with that, along with an eye-catching dance!

Animal case study

When trying to find
mates, male birds
of paradise dance
and raise their wings in
a beautiful display.

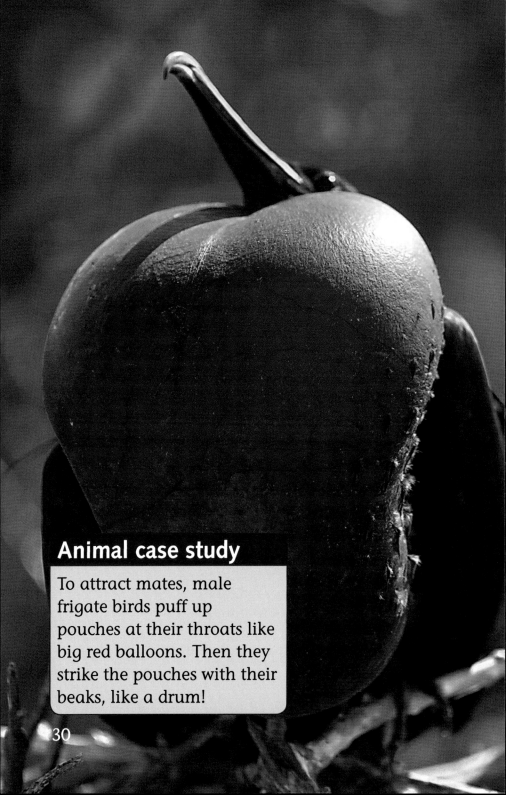

Animal case study

To attract mates, male frigate birds puff up pouches at their throats like big red balloons. Then they strike the pouches with their beaks, like a drum!

Birds are not the only animals to show off their colours. Creatures such as fish and squid use colourful displays to attract mates. Even minibeasts use colour to get themselves noticed.

Animal case study

Male peacock spiders are no larger than a grain of rice, but that doesn't stop them from putting on a fabulous show to attract a mate. They raise their legs in a dance that shows off their glossy **abdomens**.

8 Risky business

Is it dangerous to stand out?

If you're a small lizard sitting on a wall, are you safer being noticed – or being camouflaged?

What if your colourful display wins you the wrong kind of attention?

Female Aegean wall lizards use camouflage to avoid attacks from birds. The lizards are usually sandy coloured with brown patterns that help them blend in against the rocks and stone walls where they lie in the sun.

The female lizard ...

Animal case study

Male Aegean wall lizards are more colourful than the females. They often have bright green or blue patterns that help them to attract a mate.

The males stand out, but at what cost?

... blends in more than the male.

Scientists ran experiments using clay lizards painted in different colours. They proved that male wall lizards were more likely to be attacked by birds than the females.

Being seen is risky. Very colourful wall lizards are likely to be eaten by birds before they have been chosen by a mate. Males with duller colours are less likely to be eaten, but they may not be chosen by a mate.

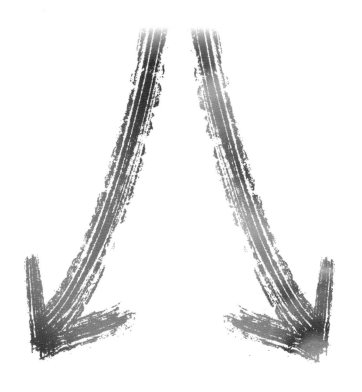

camouflage   stand out

more likely to survive

more likely to have babies

Can you think of lizards that can blend in
and stand out? It is time to take a closer look at
the colour-changing wizards of the animal world.

9 Speaking in colour

Chameleons are lizards that are mostly found in the rainforests and deserts of Africa. They have an incredible skill – they can change the colour of their scales! For years, people thought that chameleons used this skill to hide from predators.

Why else might chameleons change colour?

In fact, chameleons use colour in a few ways:

→ camouflage: to hide from predators

→ temperature control: to keep cool in the heat

→ mood: to share their feelings with other chameleons.

panther chameleon

FACT!

There are over 150 species of chameleon. The largest is the size of a pet cat. The smallest is no bigger than a human thumbnail!

Disguise

Chameleons have few natural defences. They can't move quickly and they don't have poison or a painful bite. Camouflage helps them hide from predators. Chameleons are naturally yellow, brown or green to blend in with their forest and desert habitats. They do not need to change their colours to camouflage, although it is possible they make small changes, like getting lighter or darker.

light colours to keep cool

Temperature

Lizards, like other reptiles, are "cold-blooded".
They can't make their own body heat.
The chameleon's unique response to this problem
is to change colour. When a chameleon is hot, it
makes its body lighter. When it is cold, it gets darker.
Dark colours take in more heat and white reflects it –
that's why in hot countries, most houses are white!

dark colours to stay warm

Chameleons can move each of their eyes in different directions at the same time. This gives them an excellent view of their surroundings.

Do chameleons speak in colour?

Chameleons' most dramatic changes in colour and pattern are not for camouflage or temperature control. They are all about mood.

Animal case study

Chameleons have hidden colours under their skin. A change in body temperature or mood sends messages from the chameleon's brain to these colours to shrink or get larger, mixing them together to make different colours. For example, red and yellow tones blend to make the chameleon look orange.

Chameleons use colour to send messages to each other.

A male chameleon may get angry when he meets another male, leading to a spotty display of reds and yellows. When excited at seeing a female, he can put on a colourful show. If the female isn't interested, she will darken to warn him off.

stressed

Next time you get dressed for a party, remember the animals who use colour to impress: the octopus, with its awesome display; the chameleon, with its shimmering patterns; the beautiful bird of paradise.

Do you prefer to blend in? Or do you dress to get noticed? What colours do you like, and what do they say about you?

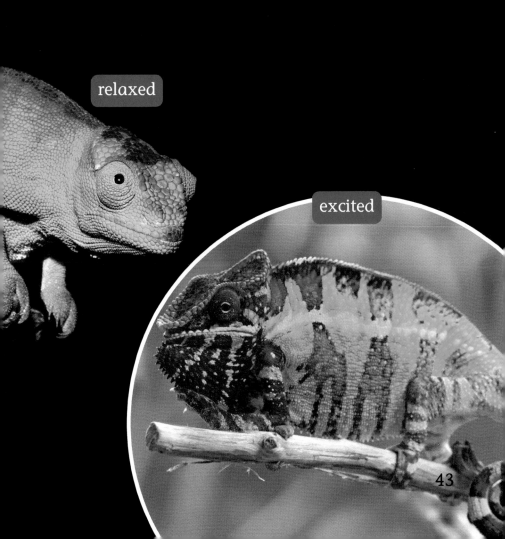

relaxed

excited

Glossary

abdomen the part of your body where your stomach is

algae a type of plant that grows in water

attractive something that is nice to look at

bushland land covered with trees and bushes

camouflage colours or patterns that help something hide in its surroundings

contrast the difference between the darker and lighter parts of something

dappled something that has dark or light patches on it

environment the place where something lives

herd a large group of animals

investigate find out

markings lines, shapes, or patterns

mate a partner for raising chicks or cubs

metallic colours that shine like metal

mimic copy

predator an animal that kills and eats other animals

savannah a grassy plain with no trees

seasonal something that happens at a particular time of year

shed when some of an animal's hair, skin, feathers or scales fall off

shimmering shining

stressed worried

surroundings area around something

texture the way something feels when you touch it

venomous poisonous

Index

Why do animals use colour?

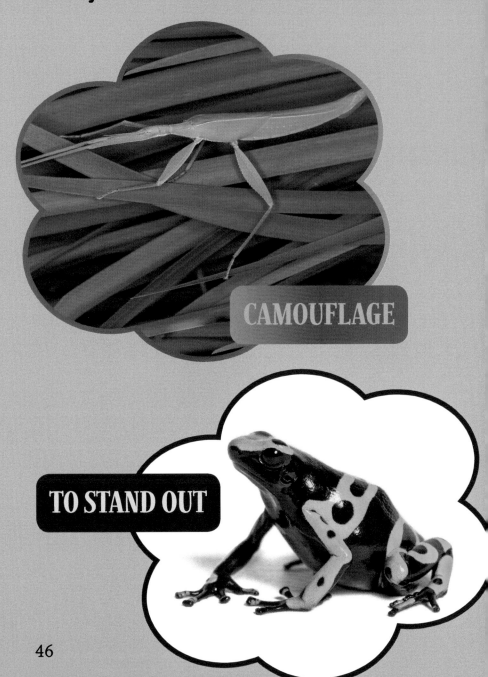

CAMOUFLAGE

TO STAND OUT

TO LOOK GOOD

TO SHOW HOW THEY FEEL

47

Ideas for reading

Written by Christine Whitney
Primary Literacy Consultant

Reading objectives:
- be introduced to non-fiction books that are structured in different ways
- listen to, discuss and express views about non-fiction
- retrieve and record information from non-fiction
- discuss and clarify the meanings of words

Spoken language objectives:
- participate in discussion
- speculate, hypothesise, imagine and explore ideas through talk
- ask relevant questions

Curriculum links: Science: Animals; Writing: Write for different purposes

Word count: 2552

Interest words: camouflage, environment, surroundings, mate, predator

Resources: paper, pencils and coloured crayons

Build a context for reading

- Ask the group if anyone has ever seen a peacock, an arctic fox or octopus before. Ask if any of them know some facts about these creatures.
- Encourage children to look closely at the front cover of the book. Ask children what creature is shown here. Play '5 in 3' – the group should present five facts in three minutes about chameleons.
- Read the blurb on the back cover. Ask the group to suggest why it is that *many animals go through amazing colour changes.*

Understand and apply reading strategies

- Read the contents page and then up to the end of page 5. Ask the group to summarise what this book will investigate.
- Read Chapter 2 together. Ask children to explain the meaning of *disruptive camouflage* giving examples of animals that use this and why.